Poetry Writing Handbook

Definitions, Examples, Lessons

Written by Greta Barclay Lipson, Ed.D.

Illustrated by Leo Abbett

Teaching & Learning Company

1204 Buchanan St., P.O. Box 10

Carthage, IL 62321-0010

Cover by Leo Abbett

Copyright © 1998, Teaching & Learning Company

ISBN No. 1-57310-108-7

Printing No. 9876

Teaching & Learning Company
1204 Buchanan St., P.O. Box 10
Carthage, IL 62321-0010

This book belongs to

_____

Dedication

All hail to our tribe of unbridled wordsmiths, language mavens, etymologists, poets and diction mongers who delight in playing our version of the dictionary game. Thanks for the wild laughter, the innovative definitions, the madcap inventions, militant challenges and lusty love of language as a source of joy and communion!

For: Mark, Susan, Eric, Lorene, Steve, Jane, Josh, Beth, Gaia, Mel, Roz, Gerrie, Joe and all the little ones coming up.

Table of

Contents

Dear Teacher or Parent,

If you read nothing else but this page (and then move into the content of this book), it is imperative to understand that we are not trying to make rhyming poets of our students! What is important is that we make every effort to help them discover the power of language and learn to use it well!

These exercises are about examining and polishing words; finding just the right one, tasting, feeling, shading, working through, listening, reciting, savoring, sweating over a challenging pattern—all the while coming to grips with the character, flavor and impact of words and how those words capture and express our views and personalities.

How do you shape your thoughts and ideas? And what does it tell the world about you?

Except when working with a specific rhyme scheme, forget about tortuous forced rhyming from young students. Most are not capable of such technical facility! Encourage them instead—to make sense—to dive in and flex their language imagination. The rewards are there for the taking. And that's what this book is about! Recalling the wonderful words of poet and author, Babette Deutsch: "On becoming part of a poem, a word exceeds its definition."

Sincerely,

Greta

Greta Barclay Lipson, Ed. D.

Remember!
April Is Poetry Month

Introduction

Students must be helped to discover that poetry is written about many things. The subjects of poetry are not limited to nightingales, daffodils, anticipation of death, a yen for life at sea and romantic love. Poetry is also about cities, jukeboxes, oil barges, cars, hunting, prize fighting, outer space, adolescence, and wars. Students need to learn well that the subjects of poetry come out of the very things that they see and know, that the language of poetry depends on contemporary and available sources for its non-literalness, that the writers of poetry include all kinds of human beings.

by Stephen Dunning
Teaching Literature to Adolescents: Poetry
Scott, Foresman and Company, copyright 1966*

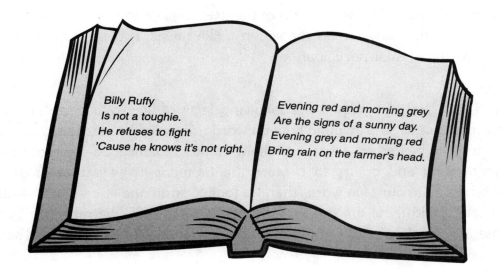

Billy Ruffy
Is not a toughie.
He refuses to fight
'Cause he knows it's not right.

Evening red and morning grey
Are the signs of a sunny day.
Evening grey and morning red
Bring rain on the farmer's head.

---

* with permission of author, Stephen Dunning, 1997.

Poetry is the language of the heart, the mind and the spirit! Each word is finely tuned to express a distillate of feeling. Each word is like a crystal held up to capture and refract the light. A word carefully chosen is a compression of thought, feeling and essence. Words witness for us and tell our stories in extraordinary ways. As with any other creative expression, the response to it is singular to each of us because poetry is personal.

In teaching all subject areas, it is axiomatic that we begin instruction on a baseline described as "where the students are" in terms of maturity and interests. This holds true on all levels, which brings me to my classroom where I was trying to explore methods of teaching poetry. My students were aspiring educators who were teachers in training and once again the principle of "interest" held true.

The topic of poetry started as an exercise akin to torture for some students who had wearisome school memories of being force-fed archaic poetry–an obscure and boring experience. They had choked on these dry and dusty archives in their young school days and were not about to revisit the rigors of tedium.

But I was motivated by the strength of the true believer that somehow there was a way to reach their awareness that poetry, like music, is a precious relevant language, worthy of their participation.

Toward this goal I suggested the following facts of life: When we are ineffably happy, profoundly sad, inspired beyond words, defeated by life, hailed as a winner, madly in love, beaten by despair, exultant in life's beneficence–we turn to the language of song and poetry to capture the moment in ways that prose cannot express! If not in our own words then we look to someone else's words–those who say it for us with lyricism and understanding! "Ah yes," we reflect to ourselves. "Those lines explain what's going on in the far reaches of my heart and soul!"

For a productive learning experience it is critical to make that connection between the subject matter and the student's world of experience and perception.

Getting Started

Culled from our collective experience, here are some "rescue" notes for teachers and students to help in the study of poetry. Add new revelations to the following posted list throughout the semester. You may want to use this or a similar list in your classroom. Here are a few guidelines.

What Is Poetry?

Poetry . . .

- expresses the music and lyricism in language
- teaches us about the richness of language and its capabilities
- defines and frames deep feelings
- is personal and can be about anything and everything
- should give pleasure and speak to the reader and the listener
- is intended to be read aloud
- is a way of seeing, translating and hearing
- is intense and captures distilled perception
- communicates on all levels of intellect and emotion
- explores the meaning and mysteries of life
- must be age and interest appropriate to be appreciated

For starters–don't get bogged down with analysis and explication! Those are more academic lessons and often make the material forbidding. Leave those exercises for more mature audiences. Don't turn kids off with poetry that transports the critics but is a soporific for the young set! There is time enough in the upper reaches of academe for those who follow their star as English majors. Encourage your students to be true to their interests. Invite humor, muscle, grit, sentiment and their experiential concerns in class selections. Remember–your objective is to foster an appreciation for the power of language and what it can do!

A Great Assignment

For a fruitful and revealing assignment, ask the students to find a poem that truly speaks to them as individuals. The rule is that they not be swayed by outside influence. Encourage them to find a personal favorite, copy it (including the author and source) and write a sentence to explain why that poem pleased or touched them. Collect these poems for insights to class tastes. Students willing to read their poems to the class are invited to do so! Plan on discussion which explores the variety of interests.

The results of this assignment can be eye-opening and fascinating. My favorite recitation came from a young man–very shy and reserved–who came to class with a baseball bat and a mitt. He stood in front of the class–leaned on his bat, turned his cap to shade his eyes and recited "Casey at the Bat" with such bravura that he brought down the house with applause!

Another impressive selection, less theatrical perhaps, was a vivid picture of a clanking, productive, noisy automobile factory in the heartland of Detroit.

In an ongoing effort, your class may continue to add to the list of all the things that poetry can mean and all the things it can do to enhance the spirit and extend language.

Why Doesn't Somebody Write a Poem About...

Add to a poetry subject list in a class discussion. Read the list carefully and make the choice of a topic that you really like. Write a poem expressing that topic. (Hint: It doesn't have to rhyme!)

Getting Mad!
Eating Pizza
It's Not Fair
Hangin' Out
The Bully
What Makes Me Afraid
Popularity
My Sister (Brother) Is a Pain
And the Winner Is . . .
Skateboard Blues
Nightmares
Grandparents
Boy! Was I Embarrassed
Being a Great Dancer
Music That Drives Me Wild
Laugh, Laugh, Laugh!
School Band Blues
Computer Madness
Chorus Voices
If I Had a Million
Gorging
Adventures in the Mall
Happy Times
My Room
Space Aliens
My Smartest Move
My Dumbest Move
Feeling Down
Space Freaks

Acrostic Poetry

Definition

In an acrostic poem the letters of the subject are written down (vertically) to form the word of choice. Next to each letter the poetic statement is written horizontally to express the subject in innovative ways.

Examples:

Me

My heart beats inside of me

Every second of the day and night!

Space Cadet

Say, kid,

Please come down to Earth.

All of us are waiting!

Could you please try?

Enough of all your weird behavior.

Can you settle down

And act human and not like a

Ding dong?

Even your best friend is annoyed.

Take off that space helmet!

Music

M y head is full of rhythm

U ntil I can barely sit still

S ee me move to the beat

I t does the same for others

C an you feel the magic of music?

Hamburger

H eavenly food

A ll America loves you

M ost especially me!

B ring your tired and your hungry

U p to your favorite fast food place

R ush to place an order with the

G ang behind the counter

E at with mustard, ketchup and pickle

R evive your strength once again!

Guidelines: Discuss the acrostic form and demonstrate it on the chalkboard. In its completed form, the acrostic should make a statement about the topic title. The sentences may start with any part of speech. Ask for suggestions for additional acrostic subjects. Try to express the topics with the entire class. Don't be afraid to experiment! Use: "Howdy," "Trouble," "Anger." Use more than one word, such as "Comic Heroes," "Computer Nerds," "Smart Alec" and "Best Friend." Reach for strong expressions. Strive for colorful impressions. Go beyond the ordinary in your choice of words and phrases.

Now You Try It

Write an Acrostic Poem

Show your poem to a friend who will help you. Be sure to edit and proofread.

_____

_____

_____

_____

_____

_____

_____

_____

_____

_____

_____

_____

_____

_____

_____

_____

_____

_____

　　　Acrostic Poetry

Alliteration

When the beginning of words start with the same consonant or vowel sounds in stressed syllables—and the words are close together, the effect is called alliteration. It takes a bit of listening to hear the repetition of a unit of sound, almost like an echo. It is a device that is used to have dramatic impact on the listener. The sounds may sound similar though the letters may not be similar, such as **city** *and* **seal**, **fish** *and* **philosophy**, **quick** *and* **cat**.

Examples:

- **Toby teaches tiny tots in Toledo**
- **Crazy cat climbed up the crooked cable**
- **Strong Sally slipped on Stanley's icy surface**
- **Mad Maxie maneuvers a mean motorcycle**

Try a class exercise using each letter of the alphabet (below) to demonstrate an alliterative phrase or sentence.

Angus the ape ate an avocado

B_____

C_____

D_____

E_____

F_____ to Z

Guidelines: Have a class contest to see which group can write the longest detailed alliterative story! You may put in an outlaw word here and there in order to construct a narrative that makes sense. Try starting with a sentence to see how far you can stretch it as in: A car–a crimson car–a cool crimson car–a cool and cunning crimson car that crashed in Carter's Cove . . . See the following example.

Story Example: **Big Benny Borovitch bakes very brown bagels on Boober Boulevard in Boston where his brother Boris opened up a beautiful bagel bakery for both him and Benny. But their bossy big sister Bessie was a baker, and she was boiling mad at Benny and Boris who baked those bagels on Boober Boulevard. Bessie was a boisterous bully with a big mouth. She wanted a big share of the brown bagel baking business! "Blast it, boys!" she burbled . . .**

16   Alliteration

Now You Try It

Name ______________________________

Write an Alliterative Story

Show your story to a friend who will help you. Be sure to edit and proofread.

Alphabet Poetry

Definition

This poetic form was invented by the poet, Paul West who must have had a sense of humor! There are many variations of this alphabet poetry starting with the wise selection of a topic. Choose one that has many possibilities such as food, sports, animals, geography or whatever challenges you. The length of the lines is your choice. Listen for rhythm and effect.

Example:

Fashion

**Accessories, buttons, caps,
denims, epaulets
feathers, grunge, hemlines,
inseams,
jeans, knickers, Levi's®,
mittens,
nightgown, overalls, pajamas,
quilted,
raglan, scarf, topcoat,
underwear, vest,
windbreaker,
Xtraordinary
yokes,
zipper**

Guidelines: There is, as you may have guessed, a problem with the letters Q, X and Z. Since there are no poetry police, you may use words that have the sounds of Q, X and Z. You may also use some appropriate fashion adjectives in place of fashion nouns, such as, *flashy, bizarre, macho, odd, outrageous.* Try working with topics such as *food, malling* or *sports.* If you select a geographic subject, select places or rivers that have strange names. You may need some cooperative research to satisfy the alphabetical pattern.

Now You Try It

Name ______________________________

Write an Alphabet Poem

Show your poem to a friend who will help you. Be sure to edit and proofread.

Catalog Poetry

Definition

A catalog is a list of items that deals with articles in a particular group. A poetic list may define the qualities of a person, a place, an adventure or anything that captures a vivid description for the reader. Catalog poems may be found in ancient writings, as in Homer's Iliad and the book of Genesis. This pattern in its most elegant form (as in praise on a tombstone) may also be called a "lapidary." It is also found in romantic and modern down-to-earth subjects.

Example:

My Kind of Friends

I hang out with my friends
Who are great talkers
Who like sports
Who try to keep things smooth
    at school
Who don't look for trouble
Who try to be fair
Who don't blame anybody else
    for their troubles
People you can lean on for help
People who don't act like idiots
People who are not big mouths
People who know it's cool to be
    smart in school!
People who do their best to make it through!

Guidelines: Ask the class to think in terms of subjects which lend themselves to lists of vivid qualities: A birthday greeting in praise of a friend, a Thanksgiving menu, a winning game, the qualities of a great day, the awesome tools on your grandfather's bench, your sister's coin collection, the things money can't buy. Keep the sentences short and sweet. Pick a punchy title for the list poem which the class is composing together. Emphasize the positive! Look up the word *lapidary*. Why is it connected to a positive expression?

I Am Not

A poem by Kathryn Mayer

I am not my hair and skin and nails.
I am not my weight.
I am not my parents,
and I am not my generation.
I am not my report card.
I am not my friends or who I'm dating
or what I used to be or my clothes or my horoscope.
I am not a gender or a diagnosis.
I am not a market or a category
or a photograph or a file or an ability
or a disability or a possibility or a kind.

But how would you know that?

From *A Blink of the Mind*
A Student Creative Arts Magazine. First Semester Edition 1996-1997,
West Bloomfield High School, West Bloomfield Public Schools, 4925 Orchard Lake Road,
West Bloomfield, MI 48323.

Now You Try It

Name ______________________________

Write a Catalog Poem

Show your poem to a friend who will help you. Be sure to edit and proofread.

Cento

Definition

Cento is a Latin word which means "patchwork." The form goes back to the second century! The objective in a patchwork poem is to put together lines of poetry, each of which is borrowed from the work of a different poet. This is not easy since the entire poem must make sense! If you want a bigger challenge, you may make the task harder by using the rhyme scheme: aa, bb, cc. However, no matter what choice you make, the syntax, the tense and the person must be consistent!

Examples:

Rhyming

1. **Those are pearls that were his eyes** (a)

2. **And the wild wind sobs and sighs** (a)

3. **We all conceive the loss of what we love** (b)

4. **The frozen wind crept on above** (b)

5. **It was almost easy to say goodby.** (c)

6. **Look at the stars! Look at the skies.** (c)

7. **My father's strength was in his eyes**

Poets

1. **Shakespeare**

2. **John Clare**

3. **Robert Pack**

4. **Percy B. Shelley**

5. **Stephen Dunn**

6. **Gerard M. Hopkins**

7. **Jack Driscoll**

(*I broke the rule* and added this line because it said so much.)

Nonrhyming

When I was but thirteen or so   (Walter J. Turner)
The clouds foretold the future of my way   (unknown)
Was it a vision—or a waking dream?   (John Keats)
In marble walls as white as milk   (Mother Goose)
I know that I shall meet my fate   (W.B. Yeats)

Guidelines: The chore of putting together a cento poem is more successfully achieved as a group effort! In order to make the project more approachable, it would be best to forego the rhyme scheme and maintain the mood and the sense of the poem! To create a cento it will be necessary to go through a couple of books of collected poetry. A reference book such as *Granger's Index to Poetry*, would be an excellent resource since it furnishes the title and first line of selected poems. The students should find an evocative first line. Each line that is used is to have the proper attribution*. Like good scholars, cite the poet (and the poem you are using if you wish). Any student up to the challenge of using the rhyme scheme (aa, bb, cc) is invited to do so! This task is so daunting that there should be a special award for any group or individual equal to the achievement!

The cento form was used to write the life of Christ in the fifth century. The poet took lines exclusively from a poem by Homer, which was even more remarkable since Homer lived 900 years before Christ.

---

* attribution: Giving credit to the person who wrote or composed a piece of work. The author. This is a very important lesson to learn.

Put Together a Cento Poem

Show your poem to a friend who will help you. Be sure to edit and proofread.

_____

_____

_____

_____

_____

_____

_____

_____

_____

_____

_____

_____

_____

_____

_____

_____

_____

_____

Cinquain

Definition

An unrhymed form of poetry invented by Adelaid Crapsey whose topics were delicate and sad! The original cinquain (sin-cane) had a set number of five lines and a syllabic pattern of two, four, six, eight, two on respective lines. As this form developed and was used in schools, there are transformations in topics and patterns brought about by students themselves.

Examples:

Line 1   **Topic** (2-syllable word or words)

Line 2   **4 syllables describing topic**

Line 3   **6 syllables expressing action**

Line 4   **8 syllables expressing feeling**

Line 5   **2 syllables–a synonym for the topic**

Creature (2 syllables)
From outer space (4 syllables)
What ship carried you here? (6 syllables)
Are you in search of peace or war? (8 syllables)
Stranger (2 syllables)

Another example in a different mood

Hi, kid! (2 syllables)
Computer mail (4 syllables)
I send it to you fast (6 syllables)
A miracle of modern tech (8 syllables)
Bye, kid! (2 syllables)

Another example enjoyed by teachers for its simplicity

1. **One-word topic** (noun)
2. **Two describing words** (adjectives)
3. **Three action words** (verbs)
4. **A four-word phrase**
5. **A synonym or equivalent for the topic** (noun)

Dragon
Fiery-wild
Growling, feeding, razing
Predator from the ancient past
Monster

Guidelines: Brainstorm topics that are unusual for cinquain as a mood piece. Think of art, music, science, math, space, history, famous women, distinguished athletes. One is forced by the rigid pattern of cinquain to find exactly the right term without a wasteful word to spare!

Now You Try It

Name ______________________________

Write a Cinquain Poem

Show your poem to a friend who will help you. Be sure to edit and proofread.

Clerihew

Definition

This humorous biographic form was named after its creator, Edmund Clerihew Bentley, who wrote the first Clerihew poem about himself. It is a quatrain (four lines) based upon someone's name and is designed to give a clue about the personality of the person in the poem. The rhyme scheme is aa, bb. Finding rhyme words for names can be a problem, therefore the writer may use the first or the last name in order to compose a rhyme.

Examples:

Ernestine Babbage (a)
Had the brains of a cabbage (a)
But she understood (b)
What it meant to be good! (b)

Chuckie Lee Stein (a)
Is thoughtful and kind! (a)
If you are in need (b)
He'll be there indeed! (b)

Billy Ruffy (a)
Is not a toughie. (a)
He refuses to fight (b)
'Cause he knows it's not right (b)

Sorenson, Dan (a)
Is quite a ham! (a)
He likes to act (b)
And that's a fact! (b)

Guidelines: This is a fun exercise using names—but remember—people feel keenly about their family names so it is not appropriate to use the name of someone in class. You may make fun of your own name as much as you please. Try using make-believe names, the names of celebrities or any you have heard that you think are peculiar and have rhyming possibilities. My favorite winner in the strange name category is the surname, Kadickle! What's a surname? What's a given name? Just for fun, can you think of names with great rhyming possibilities? (*Kadickle* rhymes with *pickle*!)

Now You Try It

Name ______________________

Write a Clerihew Poem

Show your poem to a friend who will help you. Be sure to edit and proofread.

Concrete Poetry

Definition

*Concrete poetry is visual word expression. It captures the essence of very specific words and works them through in observable physical ways. You can see **howl** through an open mouth, you can see a pop art sunflower as large as life, the word **smash** or a human struggling **between a rock and a hard place!** or **pie in the sky** floating in the clouds. Concrete poetry has the qualities of pop art in its representation of objects, idioms, proverbs or short popular expressions.*

Examples:

- **a swimming suit**
- **a skyscraper**
- **an eggplant**
- **a headlight**
- **time flies**
- **a broken heart**
- **drop in**
- **a hot dog to go**
- **a face to stop a clock**
- **flooring it**
- **a hairy problem**

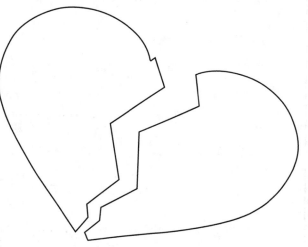

Guidelines: With the class, try first to brainstorm single words that lend themselves to concrete pictures in your mind, such as *football, steps, shaky, look, stretch* or *flag.* Expand your efforts and find proverbs or adages or bywords which are familiar and can be made concrete with illustrations. These can seem truly ridiculous when expressed in pictures: *it's raining cats and dogs, the walls have ears* and *money to burn.* Put these howlers on display with a banner that reads: *Illustrating the Language.*

Draw a Concrete Picture to Illustrate an Idiom

Show your poem to a friend who will help you.

Couplet

Definition

A couple is made up of two people, two things, two of everything. And so in verse a couplet is made up of two lines that rhyme, usually in iambic pentameter. (Listen to the rhythm and your ears will help you understand.) A complete idea may be expressed in a couplet or a long poem may be made up of many couplets (see hexaduad). These poems may be humorous or serious.

Examples: **But if the while I think on thee, dear friend,**
All losses are restored and sorrows end.

Shakespeare

Chocolate candy is sweet and yummy
It goes down smoothly in my tummy!

Twinkle, twinkle, little star,
How I wonder what you are,
Up above the world so high,
Like a diamond in the sky

Then the traveler in the dark
Thanks you for your tiny spark;
How could he see where to go,
If you did not twinkle so?

Mother Goose

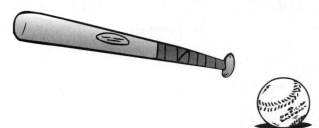

She won the crucial baseball game
Success will win her cash and fame!

Make that chili good and hot
Cook it in that Texas pot!

Guidelines: The challenge in writing a couplet is being able to express a complete thought in two lines of rhyme. With the class, brainstorm rhyme words that have many creative possibilities. List these on the chalkboard so that students can begin to see some pairs that will make a quick statement about a subject. Fit the pairs into a complete couplet statement, checking and adjusting for the correct rhythm and syllable beats. Compile the couplets that lend themselves to illustrations. Think: pack, track, back; think: troupe, soup, group; think: fire, tire, wire, higher; think: letter, better, sweater. Display these punchy couplets! Remember they must make sense.

Now You Try It

Name _____

Write Pairs of Couplets

Show your poem to a friend who will help you. Be sure to edit and proofread.

_____

_____

_____

_____

_____

_____

_____

_____

_____

_____

_____

_____

_____

_____

_____

_____

_____

Definition Poetry

Definition

This poetic form affords the opportunity to explore a single concept in an orderly pattern. The process is a descriptive one which calls for individual impressions in free verse style. The writer "defines" an image or a perception in personal terms which gives the poem its unique character. Definition poetry starts with the question: "What is . . ." Then follows a list of descriptive qualities which represent a summing up–or a definition of this important concept.

Example:

What is my flag?

    A symbol of my country

    An inspiration

    A powerful silent song

    Freedom for all people

    Justice and the rule of law

    A gift to all races and religions

    Goodness and humanity

    A source of pride

    My blessed home

    Safe haven

That is my flag!

Guidelines: This is an excellent vehicle for whole-class participation and discussion because of its personal overtones and individual perceptions. Call for topic suggestions and develop a list of concepts on the chalkboard. Have the students select one item that elicits the most interest. Begin to develop short phrases and strong vocabulary that describes the concept with verve. There will be an interesting range of reactions (as there would be if the topic were "Parents"). Some topics might be: My Friend, Loneliness, Courage, Music, Sports, Winning, Fear, Good Times . . . When working with a subject, list enough phrases so that the class can select at least 10 that are the most descriptive, lyrical and appealing. Put them in the order of your choice.

Now You Try It

Name ____________________

Write a Definition Poem

Show your poem to a friend who will help you. Be sure to edit and proofread.

Diamante

Diamante is the Italian word for diamond. This poetic form, created by the poet Iris Tiedt, takes the form of a diamond when it is completed. There are two patterns to choose from—both of which must be viewed visually to appreciate. Pattern 1 develops one topic. Pattern 2 starts out with one theme and in the middle begins to move toward an opposite theme.

Examples:

Pattern 1

Construct the lines as follows:

Line 1   **Choose a topic** (noun)

Line 2   **Use two describing words** (adjectives)

Line 3   **Use three action words** (verbs or "ing" action words)

Line 4   **Use a four-word phrase capturing some feeling about the topic**

Line 5   **Use three action words** (verbs or "ing" action words)

Line 6   **Use two describing words** (adjectives)

Line 7   **Use a synonym for an ending word**
(noun, strong word or hyphenated word for the topic)

Example 1: This poem expresses one theme about a pop singing star.

Star
Famous, successful,
Singing, dancing, shouting
Mesmerizing the adoring audience
Performing, working, reaching
Frenzied, dazzling
Showman

Pattern 2

Construct the lines as follows:

Line 1   Choose a noun as your title and an opposite word (an antonym) for the ending word of your poem

Line 2   Use two adjectives (describing words) for the title

Line 3   Use three verbs (action words or "ing" words) for the title

Line 4   Use two words to express the title noun–then two words to express the opposite ending noun. The theme changes in this line!

Line 5   Choose three action words for the ending noun

Line 6   Use two words to describe the ending noun

Line 7   Use one word–the antonym (opposite) you decided upon in line one

Example 2: This diamante expresses two opposite themes.

Loser
Careless, wimpy
Whining, complaining, stumbling
Shy, timid–confident, courageous
Stretching, achieving, succeeding
hardworking, determined
Winner

G.B. Lipson

Guidelines: Discuss the two patterns of diamante poetry. First list the "positive" subjects that would work well to expand, such as: getting stronger, a good mark, swimming, winning a contest, a new bike, a wish fulfilled or learning a skill. Add to the variety of those positive items. Try an upbeat diamante based on that list. Now list opposite subjects for a different diamante pattern. Strong to weak, dark to light, hungry to well fed, frightened to courageous, friendless and being befriended.

Now You Try It

Name ____________________

Write One Form of a Diamante Poem

Show your poem to a friend who will help you. Be sure to edit and proofread.

Haiku

Definition

The haiku is a Japanese verse in three lines. Line one has 5 syllables, line two has 7 syllables and line three has 5 syllables. The 17 syllables are a compressed form which is a composition in praise of nature. Many original books of haiku verse in Japanese are illustrated gracefully in pen and ink sketches which capture the essence of a simple moment in nature. Haiku is a mood piece in which there is no rhyme and there are no metaphors or similes! There is a rhythmic difference between Japanese and English, therefore much is lost in the translation. I have broken the rule in the examples below, regarding figures of speech, because the haiku seemed lifeless without them. This is known as poetic license.

Examples:

Old crow in command	(5)
Always foraging for food	(7)
On his daily route	(5)

A color riot	(5)
Lilac bush bursts into bloom	(7)
A splash of flowers	(5)

Ink black night cover	(5)
A wrapper of soft silence	(7)
Our way lit with stars	(5)

Water slaps the shore	(5)
Against the white crystal sand	(7)
Under a hot sun	(5)

Guidelines: Find examples of authentic Japanese haiku poetry books to get a sense of the simplicity of this form. Practice the skill of syllabication, as a class, by tapping out syllables against the desk or by clapping. Say the words out loud in unison to help the rhythmic exercise. For variations, give the class a first line only and let each student complete the second and third lines independently. Read aloud to check syllabication and appreciate the variations of the poets in the class. Enlist the skills of the art teacher to instruct in the fragile haiku art which accompanies the poems.

Now You Try It

Write a Haiku Poem

Show your poem to a friend who will help you. Be sure to edit and proofread.

_____

_____

_____

_____

_____

_____

_____

_____

_____

_____

_____

_____

_____

_____

_____

_____

Hexaduad

Definition

This poetic form, invented by Gee Kaye, is made up of six couplets. A couplet is comprised of two succeeding lines of verse, usually rhyming, with the same meter (see couplet). There is a complete story contained in these 12 entertaining lines.

Example:

That's My Hair

My hair is high and curly
It's wavy and it's swirly

I wash it and I squeeze it
I mousse it and I tease it

It's long and short and fluffy-poo
It's thick and rich and bleached so true

If I have a bad hair day
I glue it stiff with clouds of spray

It takes a lot of loving care
To tease and train humongous hair!

Brains and soul may tell a story
But gorgeous hair is a crowning glory!

G.B. Lipson

Another example with a syllabic pattern of

_____ 2

_____ 2

_____ 6

_____ 6

_____ 8

_____ 8

_____ 4

_____ 4

_____ 6

_____ 6

_____ 4

_____ 4

Guidelines: Brainstorm some likely topics with the class. Here is a chance for real humor! For practice, start working on the hexaduad above, beginning with the opening couplet about hair. Work in groups or partnerships to develop the next five couplets of this poem. Read the completed poems of all the groups to compare and contrast the compositions. Give an award for the funniest completed "Hair Hexaduad"! Put these commentaries (with artistic interpretations) on proud display. Can anyone invent an original syllabic pattern for couplets with a rhyme scheme and give it a name?

Now You Try It

Name _____

Write a Hexaduad Poem

Show your poem to a friend who will help you. Be sure to edit and proofread.

_____

_____

_____

_____

_____

_____

_____

_____

_____

_____

_____

_____

_____

_____

_____

_____

_____

_____

_____

Hyperbole

Definition

Hyperbole is a figure of speech. It is a device which uses exaggeration to give a statement impact. We hear it and use it frequently in everyday conversation and read it often in books, newspapers and magazines. It is so common that we are often not aware that we are using this technique. The good part is that people understand even though we are using hyperbole for effect.

Examples:

Hyperbole:	**I am so hungry I could eat a horse!**
In plain language:	**I am starved.**
Hyperbole:	**His face got beet red and I thought he would explode.**
In plain language:	**He got really mad.**
Hyperbole:	**This old rag–it's from the dinosaur age!**
In plain language:	**This is an old shirt.**
Hyperbole:	**I told you to stop that a hundred times.**
In plain language:	**I've told you more than once.**
Hyperbole:	**The banana split has whipped cream a mile high.**
In plain language:	**The banana split has lots of whipped cream.**

Guidelines: Hyperbole offers the opportunity to have fun backwards and forwards. Read the hyperbole above and ask for the literal translations, or read the literal statements above and ask for the students' hyperboles! With class assistance, ask for questions that challenge the talents of the Hyperbole Hunters.

For example:

- How hot was it? "It was so hot that: My body fat melted down to my ankles."
- How cold was it? "It was so cold that . . ."
- How dumb was the dog? "The dog was so dumb that . . ."
- How good was the food? "The food was so good that . . ."

46   Hyperbole

Now You Try It

Name ____________________

Write a List of Hyperboles

What do they really mean?

Show your list to a friend who will help you. Be sure to edit and proofread.

Lai Verse

Definition

The lai poem has a highly restricted pattern which makes it enormously difficult to compose. The rules are very confining but some people are willing to persevere and keep trying to work at the composition and finally produce a lai verse. The poem has three stanzas with a total of nine lines. The syllable count in each stanza is 5, 5 and 2. The rhyme scheme is: aab, aab, aab. It is based upon a five- and two-syllable rhythm.

Example:

Apparition

Are you really there?	(5 syllables)
So kind and so fair	(5 syllables)
I dream	(2 syllables)
Your vision is near	(5 syllables)
So strong and so clear	(5 syllables)
It seems	(2 syllables)
You stand by me here	(5 syllables)
And banish my fear	(5 syllables)
Serene	(2 syllables)

Guidelines: As always, your poem must make sense even though it may certainly be a little bit in the mysterious zone! Work on several lists of rhyming words that offer many possibilities such as: *noon, moon, croon, swoon, balloon, harpoon, loom, zoom* or *shrink, pink, ink, link, think, brink.* Find your way to a rhyming dictionary, which in itself can be perplexing but fun! Think about this challenge as solving a puzzle. And if you are having trouble, there is another solution: Select the last line that appeals to you most and use it in all three verses! Try it with the lai verse above.

Now You Try It

Name ______________________________

Write a Lai Verse

Show your poem to a friend who will help you. Be sure to edit and proofread.

Limerick

Definition

Edward Lear (1812-1888) wielded a masterful hand with this form and was given credit for popularizing it. Limericks make fun of everything and everybody. The lilt of a limerick is captivating and helps the listener catch on. This form is a five-line poem, written in anapestic rhythm (a metrical foot composed of two short syllables followed by one long one). Lines 1, 2 and 5 contain three beats which rhyme aa, bb, a. Lines 3 and 4 contain two beats that rhyme.

Examples:

Before we even said grace	(a)
He sat and filled up his face	(a)
He gorged on salami	(b)
Ate all the pastrami	(b)
Then exploded with nary a trace	(a)

G.B. Lipson

I knew a big fool name of Fred	(a)
Who did nasty things to his head	(a)
He tried a dumb trick	(b)
With a very hard brick	(b)
And he wound up stone dead in his bed!	(a)

G.B. Lipson

There was a large bear in a tree   (a)
Who was in pursuit of a bee   (a)
The bee was no dummy   (b)
He gave the bear money   (b)
So the bear let the honeybee free   (a)

G.B. Lipson

Guidelines: Don't be daunted! When you hear a limerick, your ears will help your brain understand the irresistible rhythm. Since limericks are often ridiculous, that will aid the class effort. An important clue to the composition of a limerick is to find rhyming words with many possibilities. Remember! You only need a set of two words to complete the composition. As a group, try to find rhyming words that can be worked into a humorous sketch. The last line, which is the summing up, will take some brain power from the entire class! Remember that limericks beg for outrageous cartoons to bring them to life.

Start with *face, grace, trace, salami, pastrami.* Do those words suggest a possibility to you? Try: *read, seed, feed, hog, dog;* try *afternoon, baboon, cartoon, monsoon.*

I sat next to the Duchess at tea.   (a)
It was just as I feared it would be: (a)
Her rumblings abdominal   (b)
Were simply abominable   (b)
And everyone thought it was me!   (a)

Unknown

Now You Try It

Name ______________________________

Write a Limerick

Show your poem to a friend who will help you. Be sure to edit and proofread.

Lune

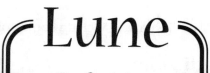

Definition

First came haiku. Then in the Sixties came an altered form of haiku by poet Robert Kelly. This was followed by a distinctly American twist by poet Jack Dollom who ignored syllables when working with children in class but instead counted words. He invented a form calling for three lines. The first line has three words, the second line has five words and the third line has three words. Some startling ideas can be packed into a theme of 11 words.

Examples:

I remember you.	(3 words)
A space creature in uniform	(5 words)
Are you real?	(3 words)
I love chocolate.	(3 words)
Like heaven in my mouth!	(5 words)
Let's eat more.	(3 words)
It rained pizzas	(3 words)
Everybody ran out to eat	(5 words)
It's crazy, man!	(3 words)

As a variation, don't hesitate to include some spillover ideas to the next line, as in:

The spaghetti boiled
over on the yellow flame
What a mess!

_____

Did you see
me on the roller coaster?
I turned green!

She struck out!
The class hero failed us
again–good grief!

_____

See the zoo
Where the wild ones gather
It's the mall!

Guidelines: List some visual topics with the whole class. Work at composing some colorful lune themes as a group. Work in teams to organize and illustrate your lunes. Display the artwork in words and pictures on butcher paper on which more rhymes can be easily added. Make a banner that reads _Looney Lunes_.

Now You Try It

Name ______________________

Write a Few Lunes

Show your poems to a friend who will help you. Be sure to edit and proofread.

Lyrics

Definition

*The word **lyric** is derived from the ancient Greek instrument, the lyre, which was like a small harp. Originally a lyric poem was especially composed for song and musical accompaniment. For hundreds of years, however, lyrics have been written without the anticipation of music. But still–these poems always express the deep emotions of the poet which have an intrinsic, lilting musical quality. The word **lyrical** is defined as "having song-like characteristics." Today, the word **lyrics** means "the words to a song."*

Examples of beginning songs:

**We were small
And made a sacred promise to each other
That we would never change
As friends we'd last forever.**

———————

**Hey, springtime is here!
With flowers and things
Sun lights up the world
And oh! What it brings!**

———————

**Do you feel pain from our old fight?
Does it matter who was wrong?
Does it matter who was right?
It only matters you were gone!
It's the reason for the song–Old friend!**

———————

Guidelines: Try to write lyrics for a song. This is the time to listen carefully to songs that are current. Transcribe the lyrics of your favorite song with a friend so that you don't miss a word as you listen. Paste these lyrics (typed or handwritten) on a piece of construction paper with your commentary on the bottom to share with the class. Do the words rhyme? Do other students agree with your interpretation of the song? Why is the song poetry? Are some of the lyrics puzzling or mysterious? Collect favorite lyrics of your class and put them in a *Popular Culture Book of Poetry*. Is there anyone in your class brave enough to sing the lyrics of a song?

Now You Try It

Name ____________________

Write the Lyrics to a Song

Show your lyrics to a friend who will help you. Be sure to edit and proofread.

Metaphor

Definition

A metaphor is a figure of speech. The word describes language that is used to compare dissimilar objects that are alike in some way. A metaphor deals with two items in a way that makes the statement vivid and strong. The comparison gives the metaphorical statement more meaning and helps make a mind picture. The words **like, as, than, similar to, resembles** are not used. (These terms are used in similes.) Strong metaphors stay in our memory because of the clever comparisons that are used. This skill is the mark of a good writer!

Examples:

Metaphor: **"Juliet is the sun." Shakespeare**
In plain language: **Juliet is pretty.**

Metaphor: **I cannot wrestle with this monster problem.**
In plain language: **The problem is too big for me.**

Metaphor: **That athlete is a powerhouse.**
In plain language: **That athlete is strong.**

Metaphor: **The campers were hungry little birds twittering at the table.**
In plain language: **The hungry kids made noises around the table.**

Metaphor: **Strength and dignity are her clothing.**
In plain language: **She is strong and dignified.**

Metaphor: **The red pop spilled out a bib of crimson red.**
In plain language: **The red pop spilled on the shirt.**

Metaphor: **That guy is a motor mouth.**
In plain language: **That guy never shuts up.**

Metaphor: **Time, you old gypsy man, will you not stay?**
In plain language: **Time goes by quickly.**

Metaphor: **Music is the honey of the human spirit.**
In plain language: **Music is sweet and tells us something about people.**

Guidelines: In the metaphors above, explain how one thing equals another and conjures up a strong mental picture. How is Juliet like the sun; how are hungry campers like birds; how is a problem like a monster; how is strength and dignity like clothing; how is spilled red pop like a bib; how is time like a gypsy man; how is music like honey?

Simile

Definition

A simile is a figure of speech which resembles a metaphor but uses the comparative words: **like, as, than, similar to**. *When a simile is used, the linking to something else is clear. Like a metaphor, the comparison of two things is designed to create a word picture that has a relationship which heightens meaning.*

Examples:

Simile: **The lie formed like a blister on his lips.**
In plain language: **He lied and it was ugly!**

Simile: **Stop jumping like an organ grinder's monkey!**
In plain language: **Be still.**

Simile: **Her brains remind me of a marshmallow.**
In plain language: **She is not very smart.**

Simile: **That player is as slippery as a snake.**
In plain language: **Don't trust him.**

Simile: **I am frightened like a creature in the pathless woods.**
In plain language: **I am lost.**

Simile: **Too much beauty is like a fatal gift.**
In plain language: **Beautiful people have their problems.**

Simile: **The horse's muzzle was soft as velvet.**
In plain language: **The horse's muzzle was soft.**

Guidelines: For practice with a partner, organize some plain straightforward sentences. Make them more colorful by turning them into similes. It takes imagination to make that transformation. On a grander scale–organize the class into teams. Assign everyone the colorless sentences to transform into similes. Who thinks up the most impressive word pictures? It can be difficult to think up the similes that have the most impact as in: "smart as a whip, sharp as a tack, keen as a razor"! How many variations and comparisons can you generate?

Now You Try It

Name ______________________________

Write Metaphors and Similes

Show your metaphors and similes to a friend who will help you.
Be sure to edit and proofread.

Occasional Poetry

Definition

This poem is just what it sounds like. When there is a special event or a precious moment such as a birthday, graduation, anniversary, wedding, athletic victory for the school, departure of a friend or good neighbor, that is the time when the poets in the crowd are inspired to sit down and write personal poems for the events!

Example:

You're Through with Us!

We're leaving you, dear teacher
For a grade that's higher up
You've suffered with us through the months
'Twas hard and it's been tough!

You're going to miss us desperately
We'll tell the world it's so
You'll sob and moan with misery
Your tears will gush and flow.

Be brave, and face the future
But we must tell you true
That when we leave this class of yours
We're far more scared than you!

G.B. Lipson

Guidelines: Duplicate the poem above as an example of occasional poetry. These poems may or may not rhyme. The class may organize into groups to produce a book entitled *Greetings for All Occasions*. Make a different assignment for each group. The book should serve as an all-purpose, one-size-fits-all resource. It may include rhymes for birthdays, graduations, anniversaries, special awards, good citizenship, get well cards and any others of choice.

Example:

February 3, 1997

Mr. Robert Balsley, Personnel Manager
Fitzgerald Public Schools
Warren, Michigan

Dear Mr. Balsley,

It's been thirty-three years at this station
with drafting and shop my vocation.
It's time to be gone
'cause this pre-mastodon
Has taught since the start of creation.

It's going to be tough to say 'bye
to all of the friends that are nigh.
I'll say it's been swell
being slaved by the bell,
but I'm going to sleep in 'till I die.

This means I'm retiring soon.
I sure won't be changing my tune.
It's been a good run
through sad times and fun,
but I'm gone on the 19th of June.

John B. Bryant

P.S. We know being sick is a bummer,
and injuries make you feel glummer.
So, in case we feel ill
and we might need a pill,
Please extend (the medical, vision and dental, etc.)
benefits through the summer.

Printed with permission from John B. Bryant.

TLC10108 Copyright © Teaching & Learning Company, Carthage, IL 62321-0010

Now You Try It   Name _____

63

Write a Poem for a Special Occasion

Show your occasional poetry to a friend who will help you.
Be sure to edit and proofread.

_____

_____

_____

_____

_____

_____

_____

_____

_____

_____

_____

_____

_____

_____

_____

_____

_____

_____

Onomatopoeia

Definition

When a word is used which demonstrates a sound it is called onomatopoeia. Probably one of the best examples of this form can be found throughout the comics where the action is captured by colorful "sound words," such as: **crash, boom, bang, crunch, kerplunk, zap, buzz**. *Many times we think the replication of a sound is exactly the way* **we** *hear it or say it, but that does not explain why the sound is described differently in other languages.*

Examples:
- **The water *gurgled* down the drain.**
- **The noisy chicken *clucked* her head off.**
- **I *cracked* that dangerous whip.**
- **We *bashed* the balloon filled with water.**
- **The little kid *slurped* his soup.**
- **You didn't cook that *mush* long enough!**

Another approach: Imitate the sound of . . .
- **a motorcycle**
- **a police car**
- **a rooster**
- **a dog**
- **a cat**
- **a donkey braying**
- **a falling ceiling**
- **crispy cereal in milk**
- **a tuba in a parade**

Guidelines: Take the most common sounds made by animals and find those identical onomatopoetic sounds in other languages! All dogs do not say, "bow-wow"; all cats do not say, "meow"; and all cows do not say, "moo"! This is a good time to explore sounds in other languages with bilingual students. Also, have the students bring in comic books or strips from the daily paper. From these the students will list the printed sounds explaining the context in which they were found. Interested students can produce an audiotape which contains a series of household sounds to identify. The class will listen, identify and write down each sound descriptively. How would the sounds be written? Write a brief story paragraph based upon the sounds on the audiotape.

Now You Try It

Write a short paragraph with as many onomatopoeic sounds as you can work in.

Show your work to a friend who will help you. Be sure to edit and proofread.

_____

_____

_____

_____

_____

_____

_____

_____

_____

_____

_____

_____

_____

_____

_____

_____

Pantoum

Definition

This form is a Malayan poem invented in the fifteenth century. Before that time it existed in the oral tradition. (Imagine how difficult that was!) Composing a pantoum is one of the most fascinating experiences in poetry. It unfolds like a puzzle as if someone else, besides yourself, was helping to write the poem. Every line in the seven-stanza poem is used twice except one line in the last stanza. The form below has 28 lines. While some courageous writers use quatrains, we used unrhymed poetry but listened with an internal ear for pleasing rhythm.

Example: This is a poem about a popular athlete in school who cannot read! The narrator asks him to be as courageous and strong off the field as he is on–admit that he cannot read and do something significant about it for his future.

Paladin*

1	**Hail to the jock!**
2	**Hero of the year**
3	**Elegant and strong**
4	**We hear you cannot read**
5-2	**Hero of the year**
6	**Incredible form**
7-4	**We hear you cannot read**
8	**Be honest with yourself**
9-6	**Incredible form**
10	**It's time to ask for help**
11-8	**Be honest with yourself**
12	**Show courage off the field**

---

* a knight, a champion

13-10	It's time to ask for help
14	Insure your future life
15-12	Show courage off the field
16	Look past the shouting crowd

17-14	Insure your future life
18	School spirit hides the truth
19-16	Look past the shouting crowd
20	The cheers will die away

21-18	School spirit hides the truth
22	Beyond the pride and glory
23-20	The cheers will die away
24	When you face the real world

25-22	Beyond the pride and glory
26	Be as fine as you can be
27-24	When you face the real world
28-1	Hail to the jock!

G.B. Lipson

Guidelines: Duplicate the numbered pattern of the poem and work on a large sheet of paper. Observe above that the repetition starts in the second stanza on line 5 where you use line 2, on line 7 use line 4, on line 9 use line 6, etc., until you are at line 28, the end of the poem. Use a pencil with a good eraser so that you can go back and change and adjust. The great satisfaction of pantoum is that you can go back and change a line that doesn't work well without destroying the entire poem. Simply replace it with a better line in both places where it occurs.

This poetic form invites the telling of a story without the rigors of rhyme.

Now You Try It

Name ____________________

Write a Pantoum

Show your poem to a friend who will help you. Be sure to edit and proofread.

Parody

Definition

A parody is usually a piece of literature, music or art that imitates an original and makes fun of it at the same time. These comic efforts have been around since the days of ancient Greece. The style and subject are usually ridiculous–and historically, nothing is sacred. Some believe that the first parody made fun of Homer in "The Battle of Frogs and the Mice." Parody can be clever and insulting, but it always makes a strong point because of its satire (which means the use of biting humor)! The best way to bring pomposity down is to make it a target of laughter.

Example: The following is a parody of the classical ode. An ode is a tribute to someone or something, and therefore the poet uses elevated language in praise of the subject. Read "Ode on a Grecian Urn" by John Keats or "Ode on Solitude" by Alexander Pope.

Ode to a Restaurant

Emporium of golden promise
What lies upon your grill
Delights for belly and palate.
Night and day you offer up
The victuals that sustain people
Of all ages marching to a gastro-
    nomic beat
A medley of fine music to all ears.
Choirs sing out your finite menu
For the lean and hungry
Who approach in reverent grati-
    tude
That you exist at all to satiate
And feed the masses.
We are humbled by your greatness.
We ask only for a chili dog,
Heavy mustard, and onions
From your exalted grill!

G.B. Lipson

Guidelines: Try writing a parody of rhymes that are familiar and you know well. Consider Mother Goose or song lyrics for an easy start. Rewrite endings and last lines of any serious poems and make them as silly as you please. You will recognize the following:

Did you ever hear of Jack and Jill
The two city kids who went up the hill,
Where Jack hung out and then fell down
And hurt himself and broke his crown
They rushed him to the closest town
In the hospital he was a clown
He refused to put on that silly gown!
Get out of here, "You stubborn fool;
You can't come here and break the rules"
Just pack your sack and don't come back,
And that's the story of Jill and Jack.

G.B. Lipson

Or invent a last line that does not rhyme but just makes a statement.

Humpty Dumpty sat on a wall
Humpty Dumpty had a great fall
　　He really cracks me up! (made-up line)

Or

I like you well, my little brother,
And you are fond of me;
Let us be good to one another
_____ _____ _____ _____ (this line rhymes with *me*)
As kindly brothers should be (original line)

Now You Try It

Name ____________________

Write a Parody

Show your parody to a friend who will help you. Be sure to edit and proofread.

Personification

Definition

*Personification is a figure of speech. This strategy is used to give objects, things or animals human characteristics which we recognize in ourselves. This technique is used to animate things with qualities which we know very well belong to people. Personification heightens and emphasizes any description in terms we can relate to. The root word **person** gives a clue to how this word developed its meaning.*

Examples:

In plain language: **Isn't that a nice small car?**
Personification: **Isn't she the sweetest little gal you ever saw?**

In plain language: **I take an awful picture.**
Personification: **The camera hates me.**

In plain language: **My air conditioner sounds broken.**
Personification: **My air conditioner is wheezing with pain.**

In plain language: **The garments on the clothesline moved in the wind.**
Personification: **The garments performed a gypsy dance on the clothesline.**

In plain language: **The cabin perched on the side of the hill.**
Personification: **The cabin hung onto the hill for dear life!**

Guidelines: When we use personification, it makes thoughts come alive and gives more power! Think in terms of ordinary nonhuman nouns. List these on the chalkboard. Now think of human actions and feelings these nouns are involved in. Ask for suggestions from the class. Some suggestions might be: old toys, a new house, a broken guitar, a jawbreaker, a diseased tree, a bowl of mush, a beautiful plane, a caught fish, a baseball mitt, a kettle drum, socks, a lawn mower, a motor scooter, a birthday cake, a wrench, a dirty dog . . . As in the examples above, give a straight descriptive sentence and then personify the same sentence.

Now You Try It

Name ______________________________

Write Poetic Sentences Which Contain Personification

Show your work to a friend who will help you. Be sure to edit and proofread.

Poetic Cryptograms

Definition

A cryptogram is something written in code. A poetic cryptogram is a lyrical saying written in strange ways that are unfamiliar to the eye. The words and letters are in their proper order, but we are tricked because we are forced to guess and work out each word. If you look up the word **cryptic,** it means something hidden in a mystery. Because we are allowed artistic freedom with the design and layout of our poems–it is our personal choice to arrange a poem on the paper in any way we please. With a cryptogram we express a strong sense of this artistic liberty.

Examples:

March comes in like a lion and goes out like a lamb.

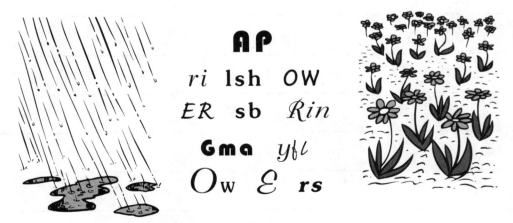

April showers bring may flowers.

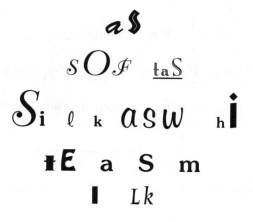

aS
sOF taS
Si ℓ k aSw hi
tE a S m
I Lk

As soft as silk, as white as milk.

AsT
IT Ch
iNTi M
eSav E sNI
N e

A stitch in time saves nine.

Guidelines: Find a book of proverbs that are short and sweet. These charming expressions have been around so long because they make sense, the language is compact—and like poetry, every word counts. Practice illustrating the proverb of your choice as you make it into a cryptogram. Add to it as many curleques, leaves, branches and designs as you choose. Use any art materials that are available: markers, crayons, paints or a collage technique. When you are satisfied, draw the final picture at the side of the words. A computer would enhance this exercise especially well. On the bottom of the paper write out the adage or bywords. Explain it.

- **Look before you leap!**
- **All that glitters is not gold.**
- **Don't cry over spilled milk.**
- **Don't count your chickens before they hatch (this can be shortened).**
- **Every cloud has a silver lining.**
- **Too many cooks spoil the broth.**

Now You Try It

Name ______________________________

Design a Poetic Cryptogram

Show your poem to a friend who will help you. Be sure to edit and proofread.

Quatrain

The clue to this poetic form is in its title. A quarter of something is a fourth, a quart is four cups and a quadrangle has four angles. A quatrain, then, is written in four verses with different rhyme schemes. It may be written as a, a, b, b; a, a, a, a; a, b, c, b; or a, b, a, b. It is a nice arrangement which allows for a compact statement.

Examples:

Evening red and morning grey	(a)
Are the signs of a sunny day.	(a)
Evening grey and morning red	(b)
Bring rain on the farmer's head.	(b)

A weather axiom

There was a man named Finnegan	(a)
A long beard grew out of his chin again—	(a)
Along came a wind and blew it in again—	(a)
Poor old man named Finnegan.	(a)

Mother Goose

I went off to the candy shop   (a)
To buy a stick of candy   (b)
One for you and one for me   (c)
And one for sister Mandy.   (b)

Mother Goose

Multiplication is vexation,   (a)
Division is as bad;   (b)
The Rule of Three it puzzles me,   (c)
And fractions drive me mad.   (b)

Mother Goose

Fuzzy Wuzzy was a bear   (a)
A bear was Fuzzy Wuzzy   (b)
When Fuzzy Wuzzy lost his hair   (a)
He wasn't fuzzy was he?   (b)

Mother Goose

Guidelines: Examine all the rhyme scheme variations above with the class. Though all of the examples are lighthearted, there are many quatrains that are serious which will match the patterns above. As a class, look at each quatrain above and tell what words rhyme in each that satisfy the pattern. What makes the Finnegan selection so unusual?

It is autumn; not without   (a)
But within me is the cold   (b)
Youth and spring are all about;   (a)
It is I that have grown old.   (b)

H.W. Longfellow

Now You Try It

Write a Funny Quatrain and a Serious Quatrain

Show your poems to a friend who will help you. Be sure to edit and proofread.

_____

_____

_____

_____

_____

_____

_____

_____

_____

_____

_____

_____

_____

_____

_____

_____

_____

_____

Round

Definition

*This form is derived from the French word **rondeau** and is called a round in English. It is a form of poetry with which we are all familiar and have sung since we were children. It is always a lighthearted verse and allows for humor and high spirits. (The formal structure has 10 or 13 lines with two rhymes throughout. The opening phrase is repeated twice as a refrain.) We moderns will hold to the simpler, looser form which allows us to sing our hearts out!*

Examples:

Row, row, row your boat
Gently down the stream
Merrily, merrily, merrily, merrily
Life is but a dream.

(New singers come in on *stream*)

Or

Are you sleeping, are you sleeping
Brother John, Brother John?
Morning bells are ringing,
Morning bells are ringing,
Bim, bam, bom; bim, bam, bom!

(New singers come in on the second *John*)

80   Round

Or to the same tune:

Granny Goober, Granny Goober,
Where are you, where are you?
Barbecuing spare ribs, barbecuing spare ribs
Yum, yum, yum; yum yum, yum.

(New singers come in on the last *yum*)

Stir that hot sauce, stir that hot sauce
Like you do, like you do
Listen to it sizzle, listen to it sizzle
Yum, yum, yum; yum, yum, yum.

(New singers come in on the last *yum*)

Golden French fries, golden French fries
Ketchup plop, ketchup plop
Tender ribs are luscious, tender ribs are luscious
Yum, yum, yum; yum, yum, yum.

(New singers come in on the last *yum*)

G.B. Lipson

Guidelines: Do have the pleasure of singing out these rounds! Make a decision about where the new singers will enter the song fest. Based upon these rhythms, have the students compose their own rounds. With the help of the music teacher, research some other traditional rondeaus, to be included in the class repertory! The addition of rhythmic equipment from around the school or house would enhance the experience!

Write a Round to Sing

Show your round to a friend who will help you. Be sure to edit and proofread.

_____

_____

_____

_____

_____

_____

_____

_____

_____

_____

_____

_____

_____

_____

_____

_____

Sestina

Examples: Ending Words: The theme of these words suggests a spooky story in six stanzas.

Stanza 1

A.	clock:	**At midnight on the *clock***
B.	grave:	**I stumbled on an open *grave***
C.	bones:	**A cruel wind pierced my *bones***
D.	creature:	**Here lay a vile, withered *creature***
E.	life:	**I cried, "Oh spare my *life*."**
F.	heart:	**I could not bear the pounding of my *heart***

Now follow the pattern for the next five stanzas below.

Stanza 2	Stanza 3	Stanza 4	Stanza 5	Stanza 6
F	C	E	D	B
A	F	C	E	D
E	D	B	A	F
B	A	F	C	E
D	B	A	F	C
C	E	D	B	A

Example of ending tercet using the suggested words above:

AB **The *clock* is stilled in the *grave***

CD **Only *bones* survive the *creature***

EF **No *life*–no beating *heart***

Another choice of ending words:

A. family
B. time
C. house
D. warmth
E. food
F. senses

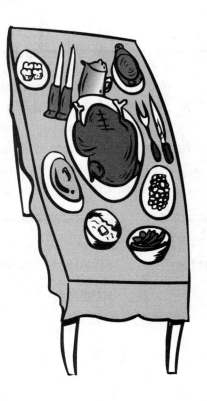

Stanza 1

A. **We join the *family***
B. **At holiday *time*.**
C. **Tumble into the *house*.**
D. **Feel comfort and *warmth***
E. **The aroma of *food***
F. **Tantalizes the *senses***

(Now the pattern changes)

Stanza 2

F. **A call to the *senses***
A. **Excites the *family***
E. **Into the kitchen–the source of *food***
B. **We wait for meal*time***
D. **Giddy with holiday *warmth***
C. **Thrilled to be together in our old *house***

Stanza 3

C. **What sets the mood in this *house***
F. **Not just the appeal to our *senses***
D. **But the generated *warmth***
A. **That flows from the *family***
B. **Never diminished by *time***
E. **Sweet humor and old country *food***

Stanza 4

E. **Bring a dish to pass with *food***
C. **Carried to the *house***
B. **And tested over *time***
F. **The variety teases the *senses***
A. **And nurtures this lusty *family***
D. **Igniting its *warmth***

84   Sestina

Stanza 5

D. **I need the *warmth***
E. **More than *food***
A. **The wisdom of *family***
C. **Fills this old *house***
F. **Memory sharpens my *senses***
B. **Through passing *time***

Stanza 6

B. **This is the *time*.**
D. **Of quiet *warmth***
F. **And saturated *senses***
E. **Dimmed thoughts of *food***
C. **A quiet tribal *house***
A. **We leave our tired *family***

Tercet

AB *Family time*
CD In this *house* of *warmth*
EF Is *food* for thought and *senses*.

Guidelines:
- Choose six key words related to a unifying theme such as cars, sports, outer space, friends, computers, the mall, art, music.
- Assign a letter to each of the six words from A to F which holds throughout the poem.
- Follow the designated changing pattern A to F for the seven stanzas with each line ending in the assigned word.
- The last stanza, the tercet (three lines of poetry), changes the pattern but includes all six words in three lines.
- Duplicate the letter pattern for each student so that the entire class may go through a trial exercise.

This has limitless possibilities in group assignments for each stanza. Good luck!

Write a Sestina

Show your poem to a friend who will help you. Be sure to edit and proofread.

_____

_____

_____

_____

_____

_____

_____

_____

_____

_____

_____

_____

_____

_____

_____

_____

_____

_____

Skeltonic Verse

Skeltonic verse was invented by the English poet John Skelton (1460-1529). It is a form which is incredibly simple and is as long as the poets have more words in their heads. The lines are short and the end rhymes go on until the poet strikes another good rhyme word to work with. It is spontaneous, humorous and goes wildly on its way! Skeltonic verse is also called "tumbling verse," and you can easily see why!

Examples:

I bounced the ball
Against the wall
It wiggled wildly up the hall
And took a nasty fall

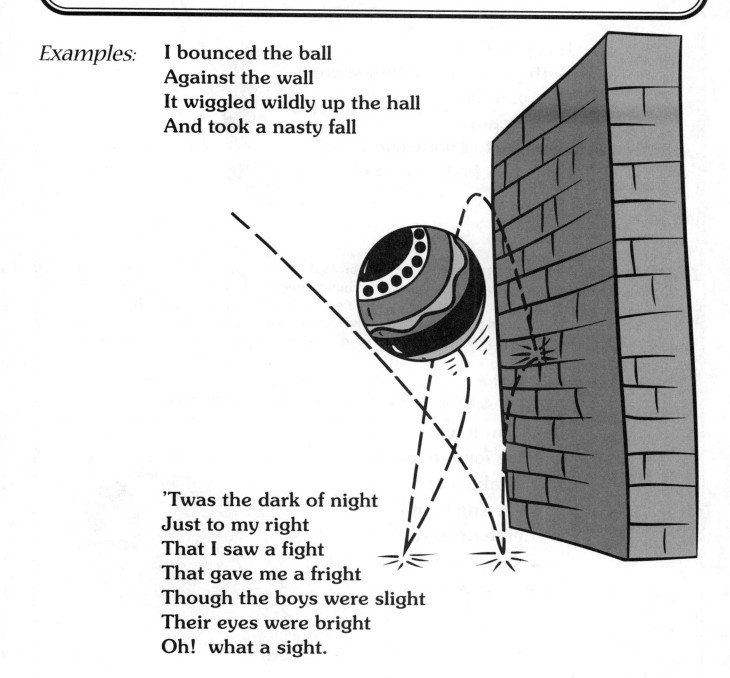

'Twas the dark of night
Just to my right
That I saw a fight
That gave me a fright
Though the boys were slight
Their eyes were bright
Oh! what a sight.

You are a friend
On whom I depend
But I cannot offend
So please don't pretend
Your acts to defend

It is you that I fear
With your long pointy spear
Can you hear
Me scream
I am part of your team
Or is this just a dream?

Guidelines: This could be a spectacular class project! It could go on for the length of a butcher paper display around the room or hung vertically. It is a challenge to focus on a subject and find the words that are versatile. You may change your rhyming words in the middle of your little verse. Skeltonic's verse is between two and five lines long, but yours may be longer. Do try to make some kind of sense relevant to the topic each time.

This is the beginning of a skeltonic verse by the master himself:

What can it avail
To drive forth a snail,
Or to make a sail
Or a herring's tail?
To rhyme or to rail,
To write or to indict,
Either for delight

88   *Skeltonic Verse*

Now You Try It

Name ____________________

Write a Skeltonic Verse

Show your poem to a friend who will help you. Be sure to edit and proofread.

Sonnet

Definition

The sonnet has a fixed form of 14 lines of 10 syllables each. It is usually written in iambic pentameter–much like the rhythm of natural speech. There are two parts of a sonnet, consisting of three quatrains and an ending couplet. The sonnet explores a subject of particular interest to the poet. The rhyme scheme is abab, cdcd, efef, gg. The summing up of the theme is expressed in the last couplet (two lines). The sonnet was invented by an Italian poet, Giacomo da Lentino in the 1200s and is one of the best-known forms in the Western World used by Shakespeare, Milton, Wordsworth and other great poets. The most popular sonnets are Italian and English, also known as Shakespearean, which will be our choice to work with.

Example: The following sonnet is about a teenager who has been out until very late at night. His parents have been waiting up for him with great fears for his safety. When he arrives at home he knows very well that there will be an argument which will end in bad feelings and no solutions. It has all happened before. The sonnet expresses both the voice of the boy and his parents.

I'm Not a Baby Anymore!

1. It was silent on our street–late at night   (a)
2. My folks in nightclothes hovered at the door   (b)
3. This was the reason for another fight   (a)
4. I knew by heart the pain that was in store.   (b)

1. Now once again they said, "You didn't call!"   (c)
2. We argued while my father paced the room   (d)
3. I told them I forgot–that says it all!   (c)
4. For them it was the painful voice of gloom.   (d)

1. "You could be hurt–you gave us quite a scare!"   (e)
2. I never meant to give them so much grief   (f)
3. These endless battles fill me with despair   (e)
4. I've heard it all before–I need relief   (f)

1. They say when I am grown that I will see.   (g)
2. I know for sure we never will agree!   (g)

G.B. Lipson

Guidelines: Often the description of a poetic form comes to life when students can listen to the finished product. Read the sonnet above to demonstrate the treatment of a topic which poses the problem and the final couplet which makes a philosophical statement. Read also, Shakespeare's sonnet for a sense of the rhythm. The more sophisticated students may be interested in writing their own and meeting the challenge of the structured rhyme scheme. In a class discussion, generate topics that would lend themselves to this challenging form.

Shall I compare thee to a summer's day?
Thou art more lovely and more temperate:
Rough winds do shake the buds of May,
And summers lease hath all too short a date:

Sometimes too hot the eye of heaven shines,
And often is his gold complexion dimm'd;
And every fair from fair sometime declines,
By chance or nature's changing course untrimm'd:

But thy eternal summer shall not fade.
Nor lose possession of that fair thou ow'st;
Nor shall Death brag thou wanderest in his shade,
When in eternal lines to time thou grow'st;

So long as men can breathe or eyes can see,
So long lives this and this gives life to thee.

Shakespeare

Now You Try It

Name ______________________

Write a Sonnet

Show your sonnet to a friend who will help you. Be sure to edit and proofread.

Tanka

This is another form of Japanese poetry which is very similar to haiku. Tanka is quite different, however, because it uses simile, metaphor, personification and more vivid images than haiku. It also calls for more syllables and is stronger and more expensive in its expression. The topics express love, nature, sadness and seasons. There are five lines in which we count the syllables: 5, 7, 5, 7, 7–a total of 31 syllables. This form of poetry dates back amazingly to 1200 years ago.

Examples:

White and silent snow	(5)
Creates the winter landscape	(7)
A peaceful blanket	(5)
An artist's windswept canvas	(7)
Falling, drifting, tender flakes	(7)

Tanka   93

Have you seen my dog?	(5)
Much more than a pet to me	(7)
Smart, strong and loving	(5)
No, he would never leave me	(7)
I feel deep fear in my heart	(7)

Gorgeous Gorilla	(5)
In a small ugly zoo cage	(7)
A tight steel prison.	(5)
It is a foul punishment	(7)
To jail such as fine creature	(7)

Guidelines: Mood, topic and syllables are the keys to tanka poetry. Call for group suggestions for appropriate subjects to be listed on the board. With the entire class learn to clap out the syllables or count the beats orally using your fingers. How precise is everyone's ear? Are there problems? Practice the skill. Pair off with partners to work on composing the first three lines of a tanka. Collect these signed papers and redistribute them to other pairs of students who will complete the last two lines. Sign these papers and return them to the original poets. Read aloud and share reactions.

Now You Try It

Name _____

Write a Tanka

Show your tanka to a friend who will help you. Be sure to edit and proofread.

_____

_____

_____

_____

_____

_____

_____

_____

_____

_____

_____

_____

_____

_____

_____

_____

_____

TLC10108 Copyright © Teaching & Learning Company, Carthage, IL 62321-0010

Tanka

Tongue Twister

Definition

The tongue twister is a cousin of the alliterative statement. These, too, have alliterative qualities but are more difficult to say. Phrases and sentences which string words together with many internal similarities begin to sound so much alike that they are hard to pronounce and separate. And so–our tongues literally get twisted. Try it and you will see what the problem is.

Examples: Let's hear these loud and clear more than once. Volunteers, please!

- **The sixth sheik's sixth sheep's sick!**
- **Rubber baby buggy bumpers**
- **How much wood would a woodchuck chuck if a woodchuck could chuck wood?**
- **Theodore made three free phone calls.**
- **Unique New York**
- **The skunk sat on a stump**
  the skunk thunk the stump stunk
  but the stump thunk the skunk stunk.
- **She sells seashells by the seashore.**
- **Peter Piper picked a peck of pickled peppers.**
  A peck of pickled peppers Peter Piper picked!

Guidelines: Encourage the students to bring in books with collections of tongue twisters or some they have heard. Have a contest to see who is the fastest, clearest, most talented twister in the class. The prize for all courageous participants could be jawbreakers from the local gum ball machine!

Look for the book *A Twister of Twists, A Tangler of Tongues* by Alvin Schwartz, J.P. Lippincott Company, copyright 1972 (in prose and verse).

Now You Try It

Name ______________________

Tongue Twisters

With a partner, find the tongue twister of your dreams and try to master it.

Triolet

Definition

This is a French form of poetry which came into vogue with medieval poets in the thirteenth century. It is pronounced "tree-o-lay," and its popularity has waned and recovered until the present day. The poem has eight lines with eight syllables to a line. The **tri** *in the title suggests that the first line of the poem is repeated three times. Envision the eight lines in which line 1 is repeated in lines 4 and 7. Line 2 is repeated in line 8. The rhyme scheme is aba, aab, ab.*

Example:

1	**I'm a guy who is always cool**	(a)
2	**I try to practice right from wrong**	(b)
3	**It's one of my firm daily rules**	(a)
4-1	**I'm a guy who is always cool**	(a)
5	**Don't ever want to be a fool**	(a)
6	**Always hope to be calm and strong**	(b)
7-1	**I'm a guy who is always cool**	(a)
8-2	**I try to practice right from wrong**	(b)

Guidelines: There is so much going on when composing a triolet that it is like watching squirrels in a cage! You must keep your mind on the number of sentences, the rhyme scheme, the syllables in each line and the first line which appears three times! It can be a brain crusher, but you can win the game! Review some rhyming words that can work into a statement. You only need two major words that suggest many other words since "a and b" is all the rhyme you need! Number your sentences 1 to 8 and give yourself plenty of work space. Some suggestions may be: *way, stay, play, day, hey, may; fan, plan, sand, stand, hand, band; night, flight, right, plight, tight* or *team, steam, dream, cream, beam.* There is a story line that suggests itself in the rhyming words above. Remember, always aim for a poem that makes sense!

TLC10108 Copyright © Teaching & Learning Company, Carthage, IL 62321-0010

Now You Try It

Name ______________________________

Write a Triolet

Show your triolet to a friend who will help you. Be sure to edit and proofread.

Triplet

Definition

The triplet is a three line poem. Though it is not as common as the couplet or quatrain, its attraction lies in the varied rhyme schemes it offers: All three lines may rhyme, the first and last lines may rhyme or the last two lines may rhyme: aaa, abb, aab, aba or a tercet: abc. In every pattern, this form makes a tight little statement. The tercet, which is also a triplet, does not rhyme. Look at the last stanza of the sonnet "I'm Not a Baby Anymore!" (page 90).

Examples:

This watch is mine	(a)
It tells the time	(a)
It fits so nicely in this rhyme	(a)

The clown didn't make us laugh today	(a)
He surely wasn't funny	(b)
So please refund our money!	(b)

Wash your hair	(a)
Comb your face	(b)
This poem has things out of place!	(b)

We knew a boy too large for his size (a)
He loved cakes and he loved pies (a)
But he ate far too much! (b)

The dragon has a prickly tail (a)
He is a sweet old thing (b)
He drives around our neighborhood and
   eats our first class mail (a)

Tercet

I mourn the loss of my dog. (a)
He was old and closed his eyes. (b)
I pray he knows that I love him. (c)

Guidelines: Think in terms of a small nicely polished gemstone! Think of a small idea that would fit into the pattern of a triplet with all its varying rhyme schemes. In many ways it is like a haiku. It would seem that this form does an especially neat job with funny themes, happy topics or serious thoughts in a compressed fashion. It would be interesting to look up some books of poetry and find this form. Consider the topics the poets chose to work with. Collect some triplets that impressed you as being well done. Record them in a book of *Random Poetic Thoughts*. Be sure to copy the source, the book title, the author, the page number and the date of publication. Sometimes you can encounter a gem which you want to remember. But without the proper information, you may never find it again!

Triplet

Now You Try It

Name ______________________________

Write a Triplet (or two or three)

Show your work to a friend who will help you. Be sure to edit and proofread.

Villanelle

Definition

*This form began in Italy where the original word **villanella** meant "farm." It was a folk song with a dance to accompany its rhythm. However, in the 1500s a French poet, Jean Passerat, wrote a villanelle which then became the strict form for this poetry. There are six stanzas. The first five stanzas are three lines each with a rhyme scheme of a, b, a. The last stanza is four lines long with a rhyme scheme of a, b, a, a. There are only those two rhyme schemes throughout the poem. Observe that lines 1 and 3 are repeated according to the pattern outlined below.*

Example:

My Mother the Cook

1	The greatest cook in the world is my mother!	(a)
2	For hungry folks we've a port in the storm	(b)
3	Come along with us to enjoy and discover!	(a)
4	I can be seen lifting pot covers	(a)
5	The aroma wafts upwards 'cause the stew is still warm	(b)
6-1	The greatest cook in the world is my mother!	(a)
7	Everyone's welcome 'cause no one's a bother	(a)
8	If you're hungry and needy come out of the storm	(b)
9-3	Come along with us to enjoy and discover!	(a)
10	Ours is a kitchen unlike any other	(a)
11	We have a great chef–just watch her perform	(b)
12-1	The greatest cook in the world is my mother!	(a)
13	When we're faint with hunger, she helps us recover	(a)
14	Like weak little birds our strength is reborn	(b)
15-3	Come along with us to enjoy and discover!	(a)
16	You can guess why we kids all adore her	(a)
17	If you let her feed you, you'll be in good form	(b)
18-1	The greatest cook in the world is my mother!	(a)
19-3	Come along with us to enjoy and discover!	(a)

G.B. Lipson

Guidelines: Some mathematicians will work on a problem that might take as long as a year to solve, while inviting others to participate in finding the answer! They might communicate with one another on the internet or through the mail. In many ways writing a villanelle can be that kind of class or group project. It is a brain crusher. Your sentences may be shorter than those in "My Mother the Cook." Listen to the general rhythm you set up to help you compose. For an easier way around this task, write down the rhyme words at the end of each line in our poem. Remember that line 1 appears four times and line 3 appears four times, which is a small help. Take your time and try to compose your own poem using the final rhyme words below, following the pattern (aba, aba, aba, aba, aba, abaa). All the a's rhyme and all the b's rhyme:

Rhyme Words (a)

mother

discover

covers

bother

other

recover

her

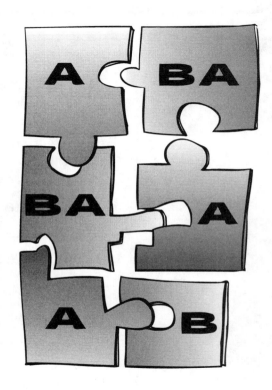

Rhyme Words (b)

storm

warm

perform

reborn

form

transform

Look for the villanelle by the American poet Edwin Arlington Robinson, "House on the Hill." Also find the famous villanelle written by Dylan Thomas in 1935, "Do Not Go Gentle into That Good Night."

Now You Try It

Name ______________________________

Compose a Villanelle with a Partner and a System

Be sure to edit and proofread.

More Activities

These suggestions may be used with a variety of poems. You and your class may be the final arbiters. Add your own ideas to this list as inspiration and class participation guides you. Do experiment! There are no restraining rules. Your classroom innovations may define a new kind of poetic form!

Plan a Poetry Reading

In the course of reading, and exposure to a wide range of poetry, students will encounter at least one poem that is very special to them. Alert the class from the beginning to be looking for that certain poem to be presented in a program to parents or other students. A few introductory comments will set the stage for the presenters who should **read** their selections. Encourage humor, gravity and a variety of moods and theatrics!

1. Collect old greeting cards for all occasions. Gather clues for the kinds of sentiments that are expressed. What kinds of verses do you like? List some of the statements that are made. What key words are affectionate and sentimental and appeal to you personally? Keep a classroom file of these cards. At the next opportunity make homemade greeting cards as a class resource.

2. Advertising is produced by copywriters who weigh the effect of every word to grab the attention of the consumer public! Some ads can be almost lyrical in praise of a product. Bring in magazines and newspapers to review. Cut out some ads that you think sound very skillfully written. Analyze and explain your point of view.

3. *License* means you have official permission to do particular things. *Poetic license* means you can write poetry in any form you choose and do all kinds of creative and unusual things with language. Design an official-looking poetic license for yourself or for other poets in the class. This should be a very handsome document!

4. Sports writers are famous for using muscular and humorous figures of speech to liven up their descriptions of athletic events. Without that poetic imagination their reports would be repetitious and boring. Look in the sports section of your local newspaper for a week and record all of the figures of speech the writers use: "Gators chew up home team; Bears put on hairy fight; Bloops and Blunders in Boston; Born to coach; Desperate Hawks fly away home; Angels spook Panthers!"

5. To internalize the feeling of rhythm, duplicate copies of "The Grand Old Duke of York." Hand these out to the students to memorize. Now apply this poem to an authentic march that the students can choreograph from this strongly accented duple rhythm! If you are lucky and have a music teacher or a local musician, it is possible to create vocal variations with movement that are spectacular. This has been done from grade school up to a college level and, like all marches, it quickens the blood and is great fun!

The grand old Duke of York
He had ten thousand men
He marched them up the top of a hill
And he marched them down again.
And when they were up they were up
And when they were down they were down
And when they were only half-way up
They were neither up nor down!

6. About one thousand years ago there was a Japanese form of poetry known as Renga which was often composed at parties. In modern times, we would describe it as a chain poem–with a few lines written by one poet who would then pass it on to another and another. It could contain 100 to 1000 stanzas and it was a fun activity for those who were up to the challenge. It can be done in class where you can establish your own rules! Will it rhyme, how many lines will be permitted per person, how many stanzas, can you link it together to make sense?

7. Write a poem in praise of your favorite athlete, singer, dancer, movie star, scientist, author, artist, teacher, coach, dentist or relative! It can be short and snappy or long and complimentary.

8. Blessings and good charms have been with humans who, from the beginning of time, have many ways of asking for protection and intervention from the fates. Somehow the lilt and rhythm of poetry helps the memory and soothes the spirit. Here are a few that should help students' efforts to start a collection and/or compose their own.

Blessings on thee, little man,
Barefoot boy with cheek of tan.

John Greenleaf Whittier

Protect me through the passing years,
Watch over me from feet to ears.

G.B. Lipson

May the road rise up to meet you
May the wind be always at your back
May the sun shine full upon your face
May the rain fall gently on your fields,
And may the good Lord keep you in the
   hollow of his hand
Until we meet again.

An old Irish blessing

9. Epitaphs, seen in cemeteries, have an interesting history. They are statements, carved into tombstones in memory of people who have died. These statements are short and sweet–expressed in prose, couplets or quatrains which reflect the writing style of the historical period. Students can create such epitaphs for comic figures, pop culture personalities and characters in literature who are recognizable such as: Frankenstein, Dracula, Merlin the magician, Scrooge, Wonder Woman and others of choice. These creations can represent a cemetery of celebrity tombstones. How about a diorama?

10. Select some short poems either rhymed and unrhymed. Organize into groups. Have the students cut apart the lines so that they are manageable. Mix up the sentences. Place each cut-up poem into a tilted envelope. Hand these out to the respective groups and have them put the poems together again according to the judgement of the group. How do these poem puzzles sound when put together? Now read the original poem. What were the problems with this puzzle?

11. Metaphor and simile poems work well with groups of four students. Working on the chalkboard first, list metaphors that are volunteered by the class: Laughter is bubbly soda, kisses and candy, mashed potatoes are comfortable, history is a crust on the world. Select one of the items on the board and add three or four more sentences of explanation to amplify the metaphor.

Kisses are candy
sweet and delicious
warm and melting
A special treat
Good any time!

12. Imagine how it would be to write a rhyme while you eliminate one vowel or consonant all the way through. The finished product is called a lipogram. Select a verse for little people or any other that you choose to work with. Eliminate one letter from the entire selection and then replace it with a word substitute. Try your best not to kill the meaning! What problems do you face? Will word substitutions work properly?

(Omit "O")

Old Mother Hubbard (The aged Mrs. Hubbard)
Went to her cupboard (Walked in the kitchen pantry)
To get her poor dog a bone: (She wanted a chewable mutt-item)
But when she got there (But when she arrived)
Her cupboard was bare, (Her cabinet was bare)
And so the poor dog had none. (And finally the sad mutt went hungry)

13. Write an unrhymed class sports poem. Vote for one sport to work with: baseball, basketball, hockey, soccer, etc. Now ask for action and fun phrases that capture the feeling and excitement of the sport. Include the fans. Record these phrases on the board. Now select the best statements and start to record them in a logical order on your paper. Include the wonderful junk food you eat as a spectator because that is part of the mood! Give the piece a punchy title.

14. You're planning a party for your friends (your choice of party). You want to make an impression on your guests so you decide to invite them with a funny poem that will make them laugh (or at least smile!) Design one of these winning invitations that others will want to duplicate and use their own. Incorporate your best art in the design using construction paper, buttons, sparkles and whatever else makes the invitation memorable.

　　　TLC10108 Copyright © Teaching & Learning Company, Carthage, IL 62321-0010

15. The following 12 lines are for an exercise called Borrowed Poetry, which is unrhymed. Borrow four (or more) of the lines below and fill them in with as many lines of your own composition. The mood and tone of the finished poem is up to you. Change whatever you want to change. Add on words before, after and in between. Give it a title.

Just around the corner there is . . .
Be satisfied with yourself, they say.
Reach out for your star in the heavens
You can be all that you want to be.
It was my dream when I was small
Would my life be more successful
Woven of quiet and secret feelings
If I could be somebody else
If wishes came true
I welcome all wonders

16. In America the Librarian of Congress appoints and announces the Country's Poet Laureate for a two-year tenure. The word *laureate* means "a person who receives highest honors as a poet or scientist." In October 1997, the year this book was written, a prize-winning poet, Robert Pinsky, a professor of graduate writing at Boston University, was selected. Mr. Pinsky is the 39th poet to receive this honor in our history. Research to discover who is presently the laureate in the year you are working with this book and learn what a laureate does. (The authorized duties, at $35,000 annually, include fostering poetry in schools, conducting workshops, enhancing the library's archives and cultivating the public's awareness and appreciation of poetry.)

More Activities

Poetic License

This document empowers the holder to use language effectively, imaginatively and with respect.

Validated on this date _____

Honorary Member

Poet's Name _____

School _____

Grade _____

Room _____

City/State/Province _____

Teacher _____

Principal _____

Society of School Poets